The Israeli-Palestinian conflict:
The narrative history of the conflicts

William M. Grantham

Table of content

Chapter one

Background to the Israeli-Palestinian Conflict

The conflict between Israel and Palestine is essentially a modern conflict that started in the 20th century. The underlying premises of the argument, which include opposing verifiable cases to a related area of land, date back millennia in any case. Jewish ancestors first settled in the region sometime between 1800 and 1500 B.C., when a Semitic group known as the Hebrew people moved into Canaan (the present Israel). Their ancestors established the state of Israel with Jerusalem as its capital around 1000 B.C. Israel soon divided into two kingdoms and spent a significant amount of time under the influence of foreign conquerors such as the Assyrians, Babylonians, Persians, Greeks, and eventually the Romans. Despite past successes, Jews generally retained their distinctive character, largely because of their unmistakably strict convictions.

The Jews were divided from their neighbors by their monotheism (dedication to one God), which gave them the impression that Israel was their "guaranteed land." However, the Roman Empire expelled the Jews from Israel after a bombed rebellion against Roman rule in 135 AD, ending the Jewish majority in that region. The majority of Jews lived in dispersed Diasporas (ethnic networks outside of their traditional country) for the next 1,800 years in Europe and the Middle East.

In the interim, small Jewish communities that had repeatedly returned to the region, along with other local people groups and a few pioneers who had been granted permission by the Romans, were occupying the territory, which the Romans had at the time given the name "Palaestina," or "Palestine" in its English structure. Palestine came under the control of Arabs in the seventh century AD, who introduced the Arabic language (a Semitic language related to Hebrew) and the Islamic religion to the region (a monotheistic religion connected with Judaism and Christianity). The majority of the population was made up of Arabic-speaking

Palestinians, though there
was a small Jewish minority
nearby that made up less
than 10% of the total
population from the seventh
century to the middle of the
twentieth century.
The majority of Palestinians
are Muslims, but there are
also a large number of
Christians in Palestine.
During the hundreds of years
that Palestine was crucial to
the Ottoman Empire, Jews,
Christians, and Muslims
each lived in relative peace
(1517-1918). However, over
the course of the last 100
years, the situation has
changed.
Like so many other current
disputes, the conflict
between Jews and
Palestinians originated in
nineteenth-century European
nationalism and eventually
spread throughout Europe
and into the Middle East.
Patriotism has the ability to

unite people from all social classes and, in any case, to bring people who live in different countries or domains together based on shared language, culture, and religion.

However, it can also be a problematic power, necessitating the destruction of global realms and leading to the victimization of strict or racial minorities. The Jewish Diasporas in Europe experienced significant effects from the rise of patriotism. According to one point of view, Jews had a greater opportunity and even pressure to assimilate into and become citizens of the recently formed "countries" in which they lived, a decision that had obvious advantages but also required them to give up their distinctive personalities.

However, patriotism also stoked antisemitism, a

European prejudice that had its roots in strict inclination but had since evolved into something much more seriously political because Jews were seen as "outsiders," impeding the strengthening of public unity. Jews responded to an increase in attacks on them, particularly in Eastern Europe, by fostering their own brand of nationalism, the Zionist movement, which emerged in Europe in the 1880s and called for the establishment of a Jewish public state in Palestine. Political Zionism inspired small Jewish groups to leave Europe and establish farming settlements in Palestine, which was then crucial for the Ottoman Empire. These settlements were initially small, and the populated areas offered little resistance to the newcomers. All things considered, the Jewish population of Palestine was still less than 10% as of 1917, and as a result, the locals did not perceive the Jews as a threat. In any case, tensions increased during and following World War One.

During World War I, European strategies, particularly British ones, played a significant role in bringing about conflict between Jews and Arabs in the Middle East. The British entered negotiations with an Arab chief to organize a rebellion against the Ottoman Empire because the Ottoman Empire, of which Palestine was a part, was aligned with Britain and its allies up against Germany and Austria. The British promised the Arabs a free state after the war during these discussions in 1915. Arab settlers accepted that their kin would be united in one vast country, which would undoubtedly include Palestine, despite the fact that the boundaries of the proposed state were rarely officially established.

The Western powers, on the other hand, had different ideas and secretly agreed to a plan to divide the majority of the region into French and British-controlled "commands." The Balfour Declaration, which supported the idea of a Jewish country in Palestine, was given by the British in an effort to win the support of the world's Jews, further complicating matters.

Generally speaking, the Arabs, British, and Jews were all guaranteed control of Palestine! The two Arabs and Jews felt that the British had broken their promises to them when the conflict was over and they took over the Palestinian Mandate.

Palestinian-Jewish ties
quickly deteriorated.
Palestinians were alarmed by
the Balfour Declaration
because they believed it
showed British favoritism
for the Jewish minority.
 Their fears grew as Jewish
immigration decisively
increased, especially
following Hitler's rise to
power in Germany. Palestine
was one of the few safe
havens for Jews fleeing
persecution in Europe,
especially as other countries
closed their borders to
refugees frantically trying to
flee Nazi oppression.
However, the presence of a
sizable Jewish settler
population upset the balance
of the local population,
drove many people from
their homes, and undermined
Palestinian efforts to
establish a free Arab state in
the region. Soon, violence

began to emerge between the groups.

The immediate effects of World War II caused the situation to degrade. The number of Jewish immigrants increased after the Holocaust, and the Allied winners were reluctant to stop them because they were horrified by the revelation of the massive scale of the slaughter in Europe. As violence between Jews and Arabs increased, the British declared their Mandate over Palestine to be null and void, handing the region over to the UN. By dividing Palestine in two, with Jerusalem falling under a different global power, U.N. Goal 181 allocated 55% of the land to Jews and 45% to Palestinians.

In May 1948, the Jews formally recognized the idea and proclaimed the creation of the state of Israel, while

the Palestinians downplayed
the region's shortcomings.
There was fighting, in which
neighboring Arab countries
supported the Palestinians.
Israeli military might was
effective. Israel's victory
allowed it to increase its
territory by 30%, and more
than 700,000 Palestinian
evacuees fled or were forced
from their homes. Israelis
refer to this conflict as "The
War of Independence," while
Palestinians refer to it as
"The Catastrophe."
Many ended up in evacuee
camps in Lebanon, Jordan,
or other areas; these camps
would later grow to be
incredibly enduring places to
call home. In the meantime,
over the course of the
subsequent considerable
amount of time, 900,000
more Jews emigrated to
Israel. As a result, during the
first half of the twentieth
century, both the population

and the balance of political power in the region underwent emotional changes.

A Persistent Conflict:

Even though the United Nations sped up the resolution of the 1948 conflict between Israel and the Arab countries, the region remained unstable. With the possibility of further conflict, the two sides developed their tactical limitations.

A large number of Palestinians joined obstruction gatherings in the meantime, disappointed by the outcast emergency and the decline in their political and financial situation. Some of these gatherings came together in 1964 to form the Palestinian Liberation Organization (PLO), which was soon led by Yasser Arafat.

Throughout the ensuing decades, Israel and its Arab neighbors briefly went to war in 1956, 1967, and 1973. Due to Israel's dominance over and involvement in the Sinai Peninsula, the Golan Heights, Gaza, the West Bank, and East Jerusalem, the 1967 Six-Day War was especially significant. According to international law, this occupation, which has persisted to the present, isn't very resilient. In addition to being several times larger than it was in 1948, Israel now ruled over 1,000,000 Palestinians. In addition, nearly 200,000 more Palestinians fled their homes (generally going to Jordan).

Menachem Begin, the first president of Israel, dispatched a mission to plan Jewish settlements in the relevant areas beginning in 1977. Numerous Jewish immigrants have moved to East Jerusalem, the West Bank, and Gaza, despite the settlement strategy being controversial among Israelis and being illegal under international law. Palestinians lost more of their territory as a result of the settlements. Additionally, the settlements have exacerbated the conflict by stationing armed settlers and Israeli soldiers inside the affected areas and severely limiting Palestinians' ability to develop (as Israeli-only access roads were built to connect the settlements, and control walls and designated areas were built to protect them from Palestinian development). Regular Palestinian citizens occasionally survive pioneer brutality, and Palestinian guerillas have retaliated by killing ordinary Israeli citizens. The dispute spread to neighboring Lebanon, where both the PLO and the Israeli military actively participated in the Lebanese Civil War. Israeli restrictions on Palestinian political, financial, and travel freedom were justified by security concerns; however, Palestinian outrage at Israeli treatment of them led to an expansion of their obstructionist tactics. The United States occasionally tried to start peace talks, but the viability of these attempts was reduced by its propensity to pay more attention to Israeli concerns. Late in 1987, there was an unrestrained uprising among the Palestinians that became known as the first "intifada" (Arabic for "obstruction" or "shaking off"). Numerous Palestinians, mostly young people, engaged in common defiance (refusal to settle charges, being placed on blacklists, striking), as well as throwing rocks at Israeli soldiers. The Israeli military responded violently, killing over 1,000 Palestinians, many of whom were children under the age of 16. Israel's treatment of ordinary Palestinians drew criticism from both domestic and international quarters. Essentially, Palestinian bombardment attacks continued to target Israeli civilians. Harmony exchanges have been prompted by the experiences on both sides, but they have only partially succeeded. Violence and strain continue to this point.

The 1993 Oslo I Accords intervened in the dispute by creating a framework for the Palestinians to govern themselves in the West Bank and Gaza and enabling mutual recognition between the recently established

Palestinian Authority and Israel's government. The main agreement was developed in 1995 with the Oslo II Accords, which also included provisions mandating Israel's complete withdrawal from six urban areas and 450 West Bank towns.

The subsequent intifada was sparked in 2000 by Palestinian complaints about Israel's control over the West Bank, a deteriorating peace cycle, and former Israeli Minister Ariel Sharon's visit to the al-Aqsa mosque, the third holiest site in Islam. It would last until 2005. Accordingly, despite opposition from the International Court of Justice and the International Criminal Court, the Israeli government approved construction of a barrier wall around the West Bank in 2002.

The Israeli government and the Palestinian Authority in the West Bank attempted to resume a cycle of harmony in 2013. Harmony negotiations were disrupted in any case when Fatah, the ruling party of the Palestinian Authority, formed a government of solidarity with Hamas in 2014. One of two important Palestinian ideological groups, Hamas was given an unfamiliar, fear-based oppressor association by the United States in 1997. Hamas was a side project of Egypt's Muslim Brotherhood and was founded in 1987 after the main intifada. The Israeli military and Hamas engaged in a tactical showdown in the late spring of 2014 as a result of unrest in the Palestinian territories. Hamas fired almost 3,000 rockets at Israel, and Israel responded with a sizable offensive in Gaza. Egypt facilitated a truce agreement that brought the conflict to an end in late August 2014, but only after 73 Israelis and 2,251 Palestinians had died. Palestinian President Mahmoud Abbas declared that Palestinians would no longer be constrained by the regional divisions created by the Oslo Accords after a wave of violence between Israelis and Palestinians in 2015. Palestinians in the Gaza Strip directed weekly shows at the border between the Gaza Strip and Israel between March and May of 2018.

The final protest coincided with the 70th anniversary of the Nakba, the Palestinian exodus that brought about Israeli freedom. While the majority of the nonconformists were peaceful, some of them raged and threw rocks and other objects against the edge wall. According to the United Nations, live ammunition caused 183 demonstrators' deaths and more than 6,000 injuries. Similarly, in May 2018, fighting broke out between Hamas and the Israeli military, which turned out to be the most obviously awful period of violence since 2014. Attackers in Gaza fired over 100 rockets into Israel before a ceasefire was reached. Israel retaliated by attacking more than 50 targets in Gaza over the course of a 24-hour period. The Donald J. Trump organization identified achieving a Palestinian-Israeli agreement as a requirement for its international strategy. In 2018, the Trump administration stopped funding the UN Relief and Works Agency, which aids

Palestinian outcasts, and relocated the American consulate from Tel Aviv to Jerusalem, reversing a long-standing U.S. strategy. The relocation of the United States was praised by Israeli authorities. government office, but Palestinian pioneers and others in the Middle East and Europe condemned it. While the Palestinians guarantee East Jerusalem as the capital of a future Palestinian state, Israel recognizes the "complete and joined Jerusalem" as its capital. The eagerly awaited "Harmony to Prosperity" plan from the Trump administration was unveiled in January 2020, but Palestinians rejected it because it supported future Israeli settlement expansion in the West Bank and gave Israel control over a "unified" Jerusalem.

The United Arab Emirates
(UAE) and Bahrain agreed to
normalize relations with
Israel in August and
September 2020, becoming
the third and fourth countries
in the region to do so after
Egypt in 1979 and Jordan in
1994. The agreements,
known as the Abraham
Accords, came more than 18
months after the United
States helped arrange for
Israel and a few Arab states
to have clerical discussions
about the future of peace in
the Middle East in Warsaw,
Poland. Mahmoud Abbas, a
pioneering Palestinian,
rejected the agreements;
Hamas

Chapter two

<u>Significant Differences Between Israelis and Palestinians</u>

1. **Security:**
The two sides discuss arbitrary attacks and indications of psychological oppression. Israelis hate that it's impossible for them to walk down a street without worrying that something or someone will go off nearby. Palestinians dislike how frequently Israeli soldiers abuse them and how their homes and possessions are destroyed when they believe a member of their family is to blame for attacks against Israel. On the other hand, they dislike how Israel thinks the land should be developed with settlements, streets, and boundary walls. Palestinians claim that such actions encourage them to attack Israel, while Israelis assert that the presence of fighters and the use of outrageous tactics are necessary to protect their relatives.

Any effort to achieve
harmony must take into
account the two groups'
desire for greater security for
their lives and property. It is
important to note that
Israelis, in particular, rank
security as their top concern.
Israelis insist that their
country should be protected
from external attack in
addition to the insurance of
people and property.
As a result, many people
believe that the Arab
neighbors of Israel
recognizing its territory is
crucial to the security of
their country and their kin.

2. **Refugees from
   Palestine have the
   right of return:**

The Palestinians believe that
all evacuees and their
descendants should have the
option of returning to their
original location, which is
one of their first concerns.
Many of them have endured

a particularly miserable way
of life in outcast camps for a
very long time, some for
more than 60 years.
For Israelis, that is the
problem; 4 million
Palestinians have been
displaced since the first
wave, a result of a high
Palestinian birthrate. If they
eventually returned to Israel
and joined the 1 million
Arabs already residing there,
there would be 5 million
Palestinians and 5 million
Jews living there, which
would alter the Jewish
population of the
country. What's more,
Israelis stress that returning
Palestinians would need to
recover their unique terrains
and oust the ongoing Jewish
proprietors.
A few Palestinians feel this
is quite reasonable;
numerous Israelis feel that it
would be inappropriate to
uproot individuals who have

been living on that land for a
few ages. A settlement that is
reasonable for everybody
will be hard to accomplish.

3. **Authority over
   Jerusalem:**
Muslims, Christians, Jews,
and Christians regard this
city as holy because it was
the location of Jesus'
ministry and crucifixion (site
from which the Prophet
Muhammad is believed to
have ascended into heaven).
Who should have control
over it, or how should
control be distributed?

4. **Israeli troops are
   present in Palestinian
   territories:**
Palestinians claim Israeli
troops harass or even attack
innocent civilians, while
Israelis claim their troops are
required for security.
Palestinians want their own
military in charge of their
own territory.

Israelis are concerned about whether Palestinian forces could maintain control over their own radical groups.

5. **Israeli colonies on land owned by Palestinians:**

Tens of thousands of Jewish settlers have moved into the West Bank and Gaza Strip since the 1967 war, claiming that Israel has a historical claim to those areas dating back to the time of the Bible. The occupation of Palestinian territory, incitement of Palestinian-on-Palestinian violence, deployment of Israeli troops, and the construction of walls and checkpoints are all reasons for Palestinian resentment of the settlers. Many moderate Israelis agree that the settlements are a barrier to peace, but they face a formidable challenge in trying to close the settlements without inciting resentment from the local Jewish population.

6. **Movement of goods and people between Gaza and the West Bank:**

For Israeli security, Israelis value the checkpoints, walls, special roads, and other restrictions on the movement of Arab residents. The Palestinian economy is severely harmed by these restrictions, which reduce trade and employment opportunities as well as make it difficult for farmers to reach their fields. The limitations also prevent Palestinians from traveling to other cities to visit family or friends or for medical care or schools. The peace process would have to strike a balance between Israel's security needs and the Palestinians' demands for more freedom and prosperity.

7. **Water:**

Water is a scarce resource in the region, and Israel controls access to it both inside of Israel and in the Palestinian territories it occupies. Israeli settlers on the West Bank abuse six times as much water as Palestinians are permitted to use, which infuriates Palestinians. Environmentalists are concerned about the Dead Sea's ecosystem being endangered by water diversion.

8. **Hate speech and propaganda:**

Jews and Palestinians are divided into moderates and extremists, and each group's extremists portray the other as less than human. The issue of words initially appears to be less urgent than the issues posed by hostile soldiers, suicide bombers, or refugees.

However, in practice, it is challenging to achieve the mutual respect required for compromise due to the underlying fear and hatred fostered by extremists on both sides.

Chapter three

Peace-making efforts

A peaceful resolution has been sought after as the cost of the violence increased for both sides. Israeli Prime Minister Menachem Begin and Egyptian President Anwar Sadat signed a peace agreement between their two countries in September 1978 at a conference at Camp David that American President Jimmy Carter organized. This agreement caused Israel to withdraw from Sinai.
Israel and Egypt had started talking, but internal conflicts

in Israel were getting worse. Only in 1991 did direct negotiations between Israeli and Palestinian authorities start. A series of negotiations between the Israeli government, various Arab states, and the PLO were held in Madrid, Spain, under pressure from the US and the USSR.

Some Israeli and Palestinian leaders, though, met in secret in Norway in order to conduct their negotiations in a setting that was less visible and politically charged. The outcome was the 1993 signing of the Oslo Accords by Israeli Prime Minister Yitzhak Rabin and PLO Chairman Yasser Arafat. Israel agreed to withdraw its troops from Gaza and the West Bank town of Jericho and give the Palestinians more autonomy under the terms of the Oslo Accord. A Self-Government Authority in these areas would eventually be electable by Palestinians. Israelis believed that the PLO's decision to recognize Israel's state in exchange was crucial for their security.

Jordan had joined Egypt in recognizing the state of Israel by the time the Palestinian Authority under Arafat was established in 1994. The Oslo Accords are criticized for failing to resolve many of the significant issues that continue to divide the two peoples.

Unfortunately, neither party ever found a solution to these problems, and the agreement's terms were broken on both sides. Israel expanded its settlements on Palestinian land, prompting an uptick in settler attacks from the Palestinians. Extremism on both sides contributed to the conflict's

continued escalation. 30
Muslim worshipers were
murdered by an Israeli
terrorist in a Hebron mosque
at the beginning of 1994, and
Palestinian terrorists struck
back with a string of suicide
bombings. The peace process
ended abruptly.
The suffering of both groups
prompted additional attempts
at negotiation in 2000. At
Camp David, Israeli Prime
Minister Ehud Barak and
Palestinian President Yasser
Arafat met to discuss ways
to end the conflict. However,
it soon became clear that the
fundamental issues
separating the two peoples
are challenging to resolve.
The peace process has not
moved forward since then
because there was no firm
agreement reached.
An additional element of
uncertainty has been
introduced by developments
over the last ten years. After

Yasser Arafat passed away in November 2004, the more militant Hamas party gained control of the Palestinian Authority just over a year later, in January 2006. Additionally, Israel has adopted a more aggressive stance: In the summer of 2006, an Israeli invasion of Lebanon and attacks against Palestinians there sparked a global outcry. Additionally, there has been an increase in Israeli colonization of the West Bank and East Jerusalem, which has led to the expropriation of water and other resources as well as the increasing confiscation of Palestinian lands for settlements and the building of walls and roads with limited access.
Gaza became the center of the Israeli-Palestinian conflict between 2008 and 2012, sparking Israeli attacks on the region and Palestinian

attacks on Israeli citizens. Gaza's unemployment rate is at an all-time high, and living conditions are at an all-time low.

As a result, the peace process has repeatedly stalled. However, both sides and international parties have repeatedly tried to restart negotiations, demonstrating their intense dissatisfaction with the current situation.

An Israeli court ordered the eviction of several Palestinian families from Sheikh Jarrah, an area of East Jerusalem, by May 2021 and the transfer of their land to Jewish families in October 2020. A number of Palestinian families from Sheikh Jarrah appealed the court's decision in February 2021, which led to demonstrations calling for an end to the forcible eviction of Palestinians both the hearings on the appeal and their homes in Jerusalem. Palestinian protesters started gathering in the streets of Jerusalem at the end of April 2021 to voice their opposition to the impending evictions, and activists and residents of Sheikh Jarrah started holding nightly sit-ins. Israeli police used force against protesters as the demonstrations grew in size in early May following a court decision supporting the evictions. After weeks of daily protests and escalating hostilities during the month of Ramadan between protesters, Israeli settlers, and police, violence erupted on May 7 at the al-Aqsa Mosque compound in Jerusalem. Israeli police engaged in a clash with protesters while using stun grenades, rubber bullets, and water cannons, leaving

hundreds of Palestinians
hurt.
Tensions in East Jerusalem
rose after the fights in
Jerusalem's Old City, which
was made worse by the
Jerusalem Day celebration.
Following several days of
nonstop fighting in
Jerusalem and the use of
deadly and nonlethal force
by Israeli police, Hamas, the
militant organization in
control of Gaza, and other
Palestinian militant
organizations fired hundreds
of rockets into Israeli
territory on May 10.
In response, Israel launched
several airstrikes that
resulted in the deaths of over
twenty Palestinians,
followed by artillery
bombardments on targets in
Gaza. Israel expanded its
aerial campaign and struck
targets such as residential
buildings, media hubs,
refuge and healthcare

facilities while claiming to be targeting Hamas, other militants, and their infrastructure, including tunnels and rocket launchers.

Prospective remedies:

The Palestinian-Israeli conflict can be resolved in one of two ways. Both options would necessitate significant concessions from each side.

According to the "one-state solution," Israel's home territory and the Palestinian territories it currently controls would become one nation. For Israelis, this presents a challenge because the state would no longer be exclusively Jewish but rather comprise an equal number of Palestinian Christians and Muslims. Making sure Palestinians have all of their citizenship rights would be a problem.

A country of Israel alongside a country of Palestine would

be the "two-state solution" (comprising the West Bank and Gaza). Jerusalem would either be divided, under joint Israeli-Palestinian control, or recognized as an open, international city as part of this solution. Both sides would have to give up their desires to rule the entire region under the two-state solution. Israel would have to relinquish control over the occupied territories and evacuate every settler from areas they have occupied since 1967.

To abandon their claims to the territories given to Israel by the UN in 1948 and likely to those taken between 1948 and 1967, the Palestinians would have to recognize Israel. Both solutions would be challenging to implement because they would call for strong leadership from the international community, Israel, and the Palestinians.

However, as global crises and human rights violations worsen, refusing to find a solution is becoming less of an option. The stability of the world would greatly benefit from a just and equitable conflict resolution.